BIRDS
OF SOUTHERN AFRICA

SUNBIRD
PUBLISHING

First published 1999

Publisher Dick Wilkins
Managing Editor Sean Fraser
Designer Mandy McKay
Production Manager Andrew de Kock

Reproduction by Unifoto (Pty) Ltd, Cape Town
Printed and bound by Tien Wah Press (Pte) Ltd, Singapore

ISBN 0 62403 794 0

LEFT *Redbilled queleas* (Quelea quelea), *described as 'feathered locusts', gather in flocks that can seriously damage grain crops.*
ABOVE *An African darter* (Anhinga rufa) *dries its wings in the sun after a fishing expedition.*
OPPOSITE *A male bateleur* (Terathopius ecaudatus), *identified by the extensive black colour on the underwings, demonstrates its aerial mastery on the landing approach.*

Introducing the Birds of Southern Africa

More than 150 million years ago, when the earth rumbled to the tread of mighty archosaurs, a small chapter of evolution started to gather momentum. The scales of some reptiles became more elaborate, in time becoming plumes, and later, feathers. The first birds had made their appearance. In time, they took to the air, and this opened up lifestyle opportunities unavailable to their dinosaur ancestors. Birds spread across the planet – from the open oceans to the highest mountains and the deepest forests. So successful did they become that they survived the cataclysmic events that led to the final extinction of their land-bound, dinosaur relatives some 65 million years ago. Indeed, for 65 million years, they have been the sole surviving legacy of the dinosaur radiations. And, with more than 9 700 species worldwide, birds are the most diverse group of land vertebrates alive today.

Relative to the size of the region, southern Africa has an unusually high diversity of birds. Although it makes up only a small proportion of the land area of the African continent, nearly half the number of bird species found in sub-Saharan Africa and almost 10 per cent of the world's birds are found here.

There are many reasons for the region's rich bird life, but one of the most obvious is the high diversity of habitats spread acros the subcontinent. These range from the dense, wet forests of the east, through moist and dry savannas, to semi-deserts, thousands of kilometres of coastline and one of the driest and oldest deserts in the world. There are high mountain ranges, rolling grasslands, huge rivers and inland swamps, and the smallest and most diverse plant kingdom in the world – the Cape Floral Kingdom of the extreme southwest. In the south the climate is mild and Mediterranean, in the north it is hot and tropical.

The region's climate and habitat diversity is not only influenced by latitude. The west coast of southern Africa is washed by the cold Benguela Current. This current originates at the edge of Antarctica and flows north along the west African coast, where its cold, nutrient-rich waters are brought to the surface by the action of strong longshore winds. The east coast, by contrast, is bathed by the warm waters of the western Indian Ocean, brought southwards from the tropics by the Mozambique and Agulhas currents. These important differences result in a dry west coast and a moist east coast. Not only does the amount of rainfall vary across the

BELOW Changing patterns of land use have allowed the hadeda ibis (Bostrychia hagedash) *to expand its range westwards.*

ABOVE The raucous call of Swainson's francolin (Francolinus swainsonii) *heralds a thornveld morning.*

region, but so too does the timing of that rainfall. In the southwest of the region, most rain falls in the winter months as cold Antarctic fronts sweep in from the south Atlantic. Further to the east and north, summer rainfall becomes the norm, much of it arriving in the form of tropical thunderstorms.

As in the rest of the world, there is a tendency for the number of bird species to increase towards the tropics. This is particularly obvious in the forests of the east and south coasts of southern Africa. Lowland forests extend all the way from the tropical east coast almost as far west as Cape Town. As one moves farther south, some of the exclusively tropical plants start to disappear, as too do some of the tropical birds. Even though the plants and birds of the westernmost forests are essentially tropical in origin, there are many fewer species than there are further north.

BELOW A foraging yellow-billed stork (Mycteria ibis) *tests the waters for food.*

Species diversity, however, is but one measure of the biological richness of a region. Of equal interest is the number of species that occur nowhere else in the world – commonly known as endemic species. Oceanic islands tend to be particularly rich in endemic species; because the islands and their wildlife have evolved in isolation, they have followed unique evolutionary paths. For example, by far the majority of species occurring on the island of Madagascar, lying to the east of southern Africa, are endemic. In evolutionary terms, however, continents also contain areas that reflect similar features to the islands. Perhaps the most obvious examples of this are isolated high mountains or isolated patches of forest.

By continental standards, southern Africa has an extraordinarily high level of endemism, both across the animal groups and in its plants. For example, more than 30 per cent of the region's reptiles and approaching 50 per cent of its amphibians occur nowhere else in the world. Birds are much more mobile than reptiles and amphibians and it could reasonably be expected that the proportion of endemic species will be lower. This is indeed the case, but relative to other parts of mainland Africa, the level of endemism remains strikingly high. More than 10 per cent of southern Africa's birds are endemic, or almost endemic, to the region. Interestingly, although the greatest numbers of bird species are found in the tropical areas, by far the majority of the endemic species are concentrated in the arid west – the Karoo, the fynbos of the Western Cape and the Namib Desert. Further east, the most notable node

ABOVE The African fish eagle (Haliaeetus vocifer) *is a familiar site along Africa's large waterways.*

of endemism is the mountain grasslands. All four of these habitats are geographically far removed from other equivalent habitats and they, like high mountains, have evolved in such a way that they boast their own, unique birds – much the same way as oceanic islands do. It is possible to spend a day birdwatching in the western Karoo and see more endemic species than non-endemic species. Indeed, South Africa alone has more endemic bird species than any other country in Africa. Ethiopia moves into second place, largely by virtue of the fact that it has high, isolated mountains to act as evolutionary islands.

Although it is commonly thought that the world's birds are well known, experiences of recent years – in southern Africa and elsewhere

– are starting to suggest that this may not be the case. For example, southern Africa is home to a world-beating diversity of larks. In the mid-1990s, 25 species were known to occur in the region. By early 1999, this number had risen to 30: and all five of the new species are endemic! But these larks were not 'discoveries' in the strictest sense of the word, because the birds were known to have been there for a long time. It was, however, only by applying modern scientific techniques, including genetic analyses, that it was possible to confirm that they were all true species. It is highly likely that even more new larks (and others) will be discovered in southern Africa within the next few years. For the birdwatcher, therefore, southern Africa is an exciting destination not only because of the diversity of its bird life, but also because of the uniqueness of that bird life.

BELOW The massive, pointed bill of the Goliath heron (Ardea goliath) *is used to spear fish weighing up to almost a kilogram.*

Southern Africa offers many opportunities for enjoying its rich bird life. For the advanced birdwatcher, that first day in the Karoo with the 'little brown birds' is an experience never to be forgotten. From Karoo larks *(Certhilauda albescens)* and larklike buntings *(Emberiza capensis)* to colourful fairy flycatchers *(Stenostira scita)* and cinnamon-breasted warblers *(Euryptila subcinnamomea)*, it is an 'endemic experience' probably without parallel in Africa. At the other extreme, a lazy morning wandering around a camp site in the Kruger National Park or in the Okavango Delta of Botswana could find you face to face with the impressive Pel's fishing owl *(Scotopelia peli)* or watching brightly coloured barbets singing duets in the trees. A short hike in KwaZulu-Natal's Drakensberg mountains can bring you in touch with majestic lammergeiers *(Gypaetus barbatus)* or the endemic orange-breasted rockjumper *(Chaetops aurantius)*.

The region is well supplied with national parks and nature reserves covering an impressive cross-section of habitats, and there are few bird species that cannot be found in one or more of these reserves. Indeed, there are several species, including many of the birds of prey, that are more readily seen in the reserves than elsewhere.

From vultures gathering at a lion kill in the Kalahari or half a million or more flamingos nesting at Etosha Pan, to hundreds of jackass penguins *(Spheniscus demersus)* gathering on a suburban Cape Town beach, a spectacular birding experiences awaits. Fortunately for the visitor, transport logistics are easy, information abounds on what to see and where, and there are several excellent field guides to the birds.

ABOVE The familiar chat (Cercomela familiaris) *is a common resident of rocky and mountainous terrain.*

The diversity of southern Africa's birds is enhanced not only by the mosaic of terrestrial habitats, but also by the diversity of its marine habitats. The cold, nutrient-rich waters of the west coast support a teeming community of plankton and fish and, as a result, are a focus for commercial fishing activities: but the same marine harvests are used by birds. Cormorants, gannets, gulls and terns abound, and several species are also endemic to the region, with the limits to their ranges defined by the limits of influence of the Benguela Current. But these rich waters attract far more than the local resident seabirds. During the summer months, migrants arrive from the north, from breeding grounds as far away as the northwestern coast of Europe and islands off the north coast of

Canada. All are attracted for the same reason – a rich and reliable food supply. Spectacular as the summer scene may be, it pales into insignificance beside the winter scenee. Scattered throughout the Roaring Forties of the southern oceans are dozens of islands, breeding grounds of ocean wanderers such as albatrosses, shearwaters and petrels. As the southern winter closes in on these islands, many species seek refuge by moving northwards, zeroing in on rich feeding grounds such as the waters of the Benguela and Humboldt currents. The wake of a trawler becomes a cloud of albatrosses – thousands upon thousands of them. Black-browed albatrosses *(Diomedea melanophris)* from the Falkland Islands, yellow-nosed albatrosses *(D. chlororhynchos)* from Gough Island and the Tristan Group, and shy albatrosses *(D. cauta)* from islands off the coast of Tasmania. Numerous other species join them,

BELOW Rüppell's parrot (Poicephalus rueppellii) *is found only in Namibia and southern Angola, north to Luanda.*

including Pintado petrels *(Daption capense)* from islands in the deep south, such as Bouvet, and tiny Wilson's storm petrels *(Oceanites oceanicus)* from Antarctica itself. The spectacle rates alongside any of the world's great ornithological extravaganzas and draws wide-eyed birdwatchers from all over the globe.

Not only do the marine bird communities vary with the seasons, but so too do those of the land and the shoreline. For species breeding at high northern latitudes, the warm weather of the southern summer is a strong attraction. Food is plentiful during the summer months and many species are prepared to take the risks of a long migratory flight to enjoy this seasonal bounty. From tiny warblers weighing only a few grams, to mighty eagles and storks, they flock south. Perhaps the greatest number of species head for the savannas, to exploit their insect wealth, but many also target wetlands, both inland and along the coast. Of the latter, many come from breeding grounds in north central Siberia, especially from the region of the Taimyr Peninsula. But some come even further. Ruffs *(Philomachus pugnax)*, for example, travel to southern Africa from breeding grounds that lie in the extreme east of Siberia, almost on the edge of the Bering Straits. This involves an annual round trip of some 30 000 kilometres! Others come from much further west – Iceland and even Canada. More extraordinary even than the ruff's journey is that of the Arctic tern *(Sterna paradisaea)*. These birds breed in the north Atlantic but, when they reach the coastline of southern Africa on their southward journey, they are still only part of the way! After rounding the Cape of

ABOVE The glossy starling (Lamprotornis nitens) *is a common and conspicuous resident, absent only from the extreme west.*

Good Hope, they continue their flight eastwards. Some only reach their final destination in the seas south of Australia. Not only is this the longest migration made by any animal on earth but, because these birds travel between the fringes of the Arctic and the Antarctic, they also see more daylight in a year than any other creature.

Whether you are an avid birdwatcher or have only a passing interest in birds, their beauty is undeniable to most and their behaviour fascinating to many. This book serves as an introduction to the feathered diversity of southern Africa – a collection of superb studies in nature seen through the lens of one of Africa's finest photographers. Hopefully, it will also stimulate many people to a greater enjoyment and appreciation of the birds around them and, more generally, to a greater appreciation of the extraordinary natural wealth of Africa.

LEFT Masterful fishers in their own right, African fish eagles *(Haliaeetus vocifer)* nonetheless readily scavenge large stranded fish.

ABOVE The tawny eagle *(Aquila rapax)* is a common species of the savannas. It occurs in several colour forms and can cause identification problems for birdwatchers.

OPPOSITE True to its name, snakes up to two metres long are the main prey of the black-breasted snake eagle *(Circaetus gallicus)*.

OPPOSITE The martial eagle *(Polemaetus bellicosus)* is the largest and most powerful eagle in Africa, quite capable of attacking and killing even small antelope.

BELOW Wahlberg's eagle *(Aquila wahlbergi)* breeds in southern Africa during the spring months, migrating north at the end of summer to spend the winter in central Africa.

RIGHT The young martial eagle differs from the adults in that it lacks the black breast and the black spotting on the white underparts.

LEFT The bateleur *(Terathopius ecaudatus)* is one of the sharpest-eyed of all birds of prey, and is able to spot even small pieces of carrion from its aerial hunting grounds high above the African savannas.

ABOVE The strangely pointed wings of the bateleur allow it to glide fast and far in search of food. As it glides, it cants from side to side – a motion unique among Africa's eagles. It was this peculiar flight pattern that earned the bird its name – *bateleur* is a French word meaning 'acrobat'.

OPPOSITE At rest, the male and female bateleur can be separated by the colour pattern on their wings. Here, the female sits to the left of the male.

LEFT The hooded vulture *(Necrosyrtes monachus)* is one of the smallest vultures in Africa. Because its bill is relatively weak in relation to larger species, it has to wait its turn at carcasses so that larger species can first tear through the tough skin.
BELOW The cape vulture *(Gyps coprotheres)* is a cliff-nesting species in southern Africa.
BOTTOM The white or pale grey patches on the inner wing of the white-headed vulture *(Trigoceps occipitalis)* immediately distinguish it from other southern African vultures.
OPPOSITE The powerful hooked bill of the white-backed vulture *(G. africanus)* is a well-designed tool for tearing apart the large, dead animals that make up the bulk of its diet.

LEFT Weak-billed by comparison with other vultures, the lammergeier or bearded vulture *(Gypaetus barbatus)*, relies largely on bone marrow for food. This it obtains in a unique way, flying up into the air carrying a bone and then dropping it to shatter on rocks below. Individual birds have favourite bone-dropping sites, known as ossuaries.

ABOVE The lammergeier is a solitary species of the high Drakensberg mountains, and master of the skies in one of the region's most remote areas.

OPPOSITE The broad wings of the jackal buzzard *(Buteo rufinus)*, a species confined to southern Africa, allow it to hang motionless in the wind as it searches the ground below for potential prey.

OPPOSITE Yellow-billed kites *(Milvus aegyptius)* are primarily scavengers, but are also opportunists. Thousands may circle termite hatches, deftly snatching the newly flying insects from the air.

BELOW The steppe buzzard *(Buteo buteo)* is a migrant to southern Africa from breeding grounds in woodlands that lie just to the south of the Arctic tundras. Each year, these birds travel some 20 000 kilometres or more to spend the southern summer in Africa.

RIGHT Resplendent in the air, the gymnogene *(Polyboroides typus)* is a highly specialized predator. Its ankle joint (the joint in the middle of the exposed leg) is uniquely double-jointed, allowing it to perform extraordinary contortions while trying to extract the young of hole-nesting birds from their refuges.

BOTTOM RIGHT Black-shouldered kites *(Elanus caeruleus)* are found throughout most of southern Africa. The white tips to the dark upperpart feathers identify this bird as a juvenile – it can be seen performing the very characteristic tail-raising of this species.

LEFT The little sparrowhawk *(Accipiter minullus)* is a rather inconspicuous bird of thick woodlands, usually affording the observer little more than a glimpse of a bullet-like flash of grey as it dashes from tree to tree.

ABOVE Plantations of exotic trees have enabled the Ovambo sparrowhawk *(A. ovampensis)* to increase its range, especially in South Africa.

OPPOSITE Long-tailed and long-winged, the African marsh harrier *(Circus ranivorus)* lives in large wetlands. Here it flies low and slowly above the vegetation, suddenly dropping from sight as it spies prey on the ground below.

TOP LEFT Less specialised than the closely related peregrine falcon *(Falco peregrinus)*, in some areas lanner falcons *(F. biarmicus)* subsist largely on a diet of free-ranging chickens.

LEFT The lanner falcon is primarily a cliff-nester, but it is an opportunistic species, sometimes taking over disused crows' nests as breeding sites.

ABOVE The pygmy falcon *(Polihierax semitorquatus)*, particularly common in the southern Kalahari, is no bigger than a shrike and is the smallest bird of prey in Africa.

OPPOSITE The giant nests of the sociable weaver *(Philetairus socius)* are also the nesting site of the pygmy falcon. The falcons nest in a chamber within the thatch dome, but are not molested by the weavers – possibly because they provide some protection from potential nest-robbers such as snakes.

ABOVE The pale chanting goshawk *(Melierax canorus)* of the dry west has an interesting association with the African honey badger. As the honey badger grubs for food among the roots of bushes, the goshawks wait nearby, ready to pounce on unsuspecting rodents fleeing the disturbance created by the honey badger.

ABOVE Gabar goshawks *(Micronisus gabar)* frequently perch motionless in trees at waterholes, waiting for a lapse in concentration among the smaller birds drinking below.

OPPOSITE Rock kestrels *(Falco tinnunculus)* are common and widespread in southern Africa. Like their close relatives elsewhere in the world, they have adapted fairly well to living with humankind, regularly using buildings as a substitute for more natural, cliff-face nest sites.

OPPOSITE Round-eyed hunters of the wetland nights, marsh owls (Asio capensis) hide in dense marshy vegetation during the day, emerging at dusk in search of rodents and birds.

ABOVE The pearl-spotted owl *(Glaucidium perlatum)* is among the smallest and most diurnal of Africa's owls. An inveterate nest-robber, its presence is often revealed by its far-carrying rising and falling whistling call. Small birds respond rapidly to this sound, searching for and then mobbing the owl.

RIGHT Strictly nocturnal, the huge, black-eyed Pel's fishing owl *(Scotopelia peli)* hunts from branches overhanging slow-moving tropical rivers. At the sight of a fish below, it drops silently from its perch and then returns with its catch to a favoured feeding site in a large tree.

ABOVE The medium-sized marsh owl *(Asio capensis)* tends to prefer marshes and damp grassland and avoids wetland areas that have become overgrown with reeds. This rather plain owl has a patchy distribution in Morocco, sub-Saharan Africa and Madagascar, and may on occasion be found in flocks.

ABOVE The drooping pink eyelids of a sleepy giant eagle owl *(Bubo lacteus)* belie the predatory power of the largest owl in southern Africa. It may swoop on prey as large as monkeys. OPPOSITE Despite their large size, giant eagle owls can be difficult to spot during the day as they retreat deep into the shade of a large tree, hiding from the sun until darkness falls.

LEFT The spotted eagle owl *(Bubo africanus)* is the region's most widespread and abundant eagle owl. Less powerful than its larger relatives, it preys mostly on invertebrates.

ABOVE Spotted eagle owls nest on the ground, in trees or on cliffs. The parent birds are very devoted to their young and are quite likely to make a physical attack on human and other intruders at the nest.

OPPOSITE The nocturnal hunting habits of the spotted eagle owl – like all owls – require special adaptations of the eye, both in terms of its shape and its nervous structure. Owls' retinas are rich in rods, allowing them to see in very low light conditions – but at the expense of good colour vision.

LEFT The ostrich *(Struthio camelus)* is not only the largest living bird, but it also has the largest eye of any terrestrial vertebrate.

BELOW The long, powerful legs of the secretarybird *(Sagittarius serpentarius)* are used to stamp on its insect and reptile prey. After the prey is killed or stunned, it is swallowed whole.

BOTTOM Ostriches have close relatives in South America, Australia and New Zealand. These all arose from a common ancestor that evolved before the break-up of Gondwana.

OPPOSITE The secretarybird's name derives from black, quill-like feathers on the back of its head.

PREVIOUS PAGE, LEFT The massive southern ground hornbill *(Bucorvus leadbeateri)* lives in family groups. These birds have a very low reproductive rate, but when they do have chicks, young from previous broods help to feed them. The young can be dependent on their parents for food for as long as a year.

PREVIOUS PAGE, RIGHT The large and apparently unwieldy bill of the southern ground hornbill is surprisingly well adapted for coping with its exclusively carnivorous diet.

TOP LEFT The northern black korhaan *(Eupodotis afraoides)* has only recently been recognised as being a distinct species from its southern relative *E. afra*, the latter being confined to fynbos habitats.

LEFT During the breeding season, the male northern black korhaan indulges in noisy and raucous vocal displays, sometimes adding to the effect with a display flight ending in a parachuting glide with the legs held down.

ABOVE Africa's heaviest flying bird, the haughty Kori bustard *(Ardeotis kori)* struts its way across the open drylands of southern Africa. Unfortunately, habitat loss, poisoning and hunting have taken their toll, and the species' numbers and range are both much reduced.

OPPOSITE The Afrikaans name for the Kori bustard is *gompou*, meaning 'gum fowl'. This comes from its habit of eating the resin that seeps from the trunks of acacia trees.

LEFT The Natal francolin *(Francolinus natalensis)* is a woodland species that, in some parts of its range, has benefitted from bush encroachment caused by overgrazing.

TOP The raucous, staccato call of the red-billed francolin *(F. adspersus)* is one of the most familiar dawn and dusk sounds in Namibia and Botswana

ABOVE Crested francolins *(F. sephaena)* are found in groups in woodland and forest. At dusk, they fly up into trees and bushes where they spend the night to avoid ground predators.

OPPOSITE The Cape francolin *(F. capensis)* is confined to the western areas of South Africa, where it may become very tame around human habitation, even flying onto picnic tables in search of scraps.

LEFT The helmeted guineafowl *(Numida meleagris)* is found almost throughout southern Africa. In many places, wild birds have hybridized with domestic guineafowl, producing a genetic pot-pourri.

ABOVE The crest and facial markings of helmeted guineafowl vary in different parts of Africa and are the easiest means of identifying the different subspecies.

OPPOSITE Unlike the noisy and conspicuous helmeted guineafowl, the crested guineafowl *(Guttera pucherani)* is a secretive species of forests and thickets. Fruits are prominent on their menu and they sometimes follow troops of foraging monkeys to glean their discards.

OPPOSITE The female double-banded sandgrouse *(Pterocles bicintus)* is much more camouflaged than her mate. Usually seen in pairs during the day, huge numbers of these birds congregate to drink at waterholes at dusk and just after.

ABOVE Namaqua sandgrouse *(P. namaqua)* breed in the arid west of the region. On average, their breeding success is low because many nests are lost to predators such as mongooses and snakes.

RIGHT Sandgrouse have to fly to drinking points daily and, like other sandgrouse species, Burchell's sandgrouse *(P. burchelli)* has specially adapted feathers on its belly with which it can transport water back to its young.

ABOVE Water dikkops *(Burhinus vermiculatus)*, as their name suggests, occur at wetlands, along rivers and even on open beaches. Like other shorebirds, they lay their eggs in a simple scrape on the ground. They are very aggressive when defending of their nests and young, and will even tackle intruders as large as crocodiles. They can easily be distinguished from the closely related spotted dikkop *(B. capensis)* by the pale band on the folded wing.

ABOVE Dikkops are predominantly nocturnal foragers. By shorebird standards, they are large and powerful and the spotted dikkop shown here will tackle an array of prey, including snakes.

OPPOSITE During the daylight hours, spotted dikkops rest under the shelter of a bush or tree. As night begins to fall, they become active, and their piercing whistling calls – often given in flight – carry long distances.

TOP LEFT The stately blue crane *(Anthropoides paradiseus)* is South Africa's national bird. Outside the country's borders, there is only one small population confined to Etosha National Park in Namibia.
LEFT By far the largest crane in southern Africa, the stately wattled crane *(Grus carunculatus)* is very sensitive to the degradation of its wetland habitat. The crane's range and numbers have greatly decreased in recent times and conservation is an urgent priority.
ABOVE Blue cranes regularly converge on recently planted crops to feed. This brings them into conflict with farmers and poisoning still occurs on agricultural land.
OPPOSITE The striking head plumes and facial pattern of the southern crowned crane *(Balearica regulorum)* render this bird unmistakable. At the onset of the breeding season, southern crowned cranes perform elaborate dances, bouncing and pirouetting together with their wings outstretched.

TOP LEFT Short, wet grasslands and marshland fringes are the home of the wattled plover *(Vanellus senegallus)*. Like crowned *(V. coronatus)* and blacksmith *(V. armatus)* plovers, this species has adapted fairly well to living in city suburbs.

LEFT The uncommon black-winged plover *(V. melanopterus)* is found in short and burnt grasslands. They fly extensively at night, probably to locate active burns. Black-winged plovers may join forces with crowned plovers when searching for food.

ABOVE The crowned plover is one of the best-known grassland birds of Africa. Noisy, conspicuous and unafraid, it regularly lives in association with humankind, favouring golf courses, sports fields and parks.

OPPOSITE In defence of their eggs and young, crowned plovers show no fear and will display vigorously and noisily in front of people, livestock and even vehicles.

OPPOSITE The contrasting, monochromatic plumage of the blacksmith plover is a warning signal to predators that it is distasteful. Sometimes, when predators approach, the birds spread their wings to display their warning signal more conspicuously.

BELOW The blacksmith plover's name derives from its distinctive call: sharp, explosive notes that sound much like a blacksmith striking an anvil.

RIGHT Kittlitz's plovers *(Charadrius pecuarius)* favour natural pans as well as man-made wetlands and heavily grazed lands. Their movement patterns, in response to rainfall, are both complex and unpredictable.

BOTTOM RIGHT Three-banded plovers *(C. tricollaris)* often breed on open muddy or shingle banks close to water. Because the eggs are laid on the ground, they are extraordinarily well camouflaged and difficult to see.

LEFT The strange, upturned bill of the pied avocet *(Recurvirostra avosetta)* is a special adaptation to its method of feeding. The bill is swept from side to side in the water, just brushing the mud surface. Sensory cells in the bill allow the bird to detect its small invertebrate prey.

ABOVE Closely related to the avocets, the black-winged stilt *(Himantopus himantopus)* has a straight bill resembling a pair of forceps. This it uses to pick tiny prey from the water or mud surface.

OPPOSITE The long, robust bill of the Ethiopian snipe *(Gallinago nigripennis)* is pushed deep into soft mud in search of worms and other buried food. These birds have specially structured outer tail feathers that are spread during fast aerial displays. As the air passes over the feathers, it creates a characteristic 'drumming' sound.

LEFT Common sandpipers *(Actitis hypoleucos)* migrate to Africa from breeding grounds in Europe. While here they are usually found along rivers and at freshwater wetlands. When foraging, they continuously bob their tails like a wagtail.

BELOW The ruff *(Philomachus pugnax)* is one of the longest-distance migrants to visit southern Africa. Most of these birds come from breeding grounds in the far east of Siberia, undertaking an annual migration of some 30 000 kilometres. In southern Africa, the smaller females outnumber males by about eight to one.

OPPOSITE The wood sandpiper *(Tringa glareola)* is another migrant from northern breeding grounds. It is a very common wader throughout much of the interior of Africa, favouring marshes and other freshwater wetlands.

TOP LEFT The massive, irridescent purple gallinule *(Porphyrio Porphyrio)* is a marshland specialist. It feeds mostly on the corms of water plants, which it holds in its huge feet while tearing them apart with its bill – although it is also not averse to robbing the occasional nest of its contents.

LEFT The African rail *(Rallus caerulescens)* is a common, but secretive, reedbed-dweller. Its presence is most often given away by its piercing, trilling song.

ABOVE The black crake *(Amaurornis flavirostris)* is a shy inhabitant of reedbeds and rank marshes. Most active at dawn and dusk, it is often first located by its complex, wheezing duet.

OPPOSITE The female African jacana *(Actophilornis africanus)* is much larger than the male of the species. A female jacana will mate with several males in succession, laying a clutch of eggs for each one. After the female has laid the eggs, it is the male who is entirely responsible for their incubation and the rearing of the chicks. This breeding system, known as polyandry, occurs in fewer than 20 species of bird in the world.

LEFT The cattle egret *(Bubulcus ibis)* has undergone a massive range extension, expanding from Africa to both South and North America, and from Asia as far east as Australia.
BELOW Black-crowned night herons *(Nycticorax nycticorax)* are nocturnal, but conspicuous in the breeding season when they frequently nest in association with other diurnal species.
BELOW BOTTOM The great white egret *(Casmerodius albus)* is Africa's largest egret. The yellow bill indicates that it is not breeding: during the breeding season, the bill is black.
OPPOSITE The grey heron *(Ardea purpurea)* is widely distributed in the Old World. It is a 'sit-and-wait' predator, waiting for a fish or frog to swim within range of its lethal bill.

Opposite The little bittern *(Ixobrychus minutus)* is a skulking inhabitant of tall reedbeds. Two races occur in southern Africa, one of which is a breeding resident and the other a non-breeding migrant from further north.

Above The common squacco heron *(Ardeola ralloides)* is a widespread and conspicuous resident of tropical and sub-tropical wetlands. It works its way along the wetland margins in search of frogs and large invertebrates.

Right The uniform colour of the black egret *(Egretta ardesiaca)* is broken only by its bright yellow feet. This bird displays a unique foraging behaviour in which it speads its wings out and forwards, forming an umbrella with the head pointing downwards in the centre. Precisely what benefit it derives from this is still uncertain.

Overleaf, left The green-backed heron *(Butorides striatus)* is a stealthy predator of shore margins, inching forwards centimetre by centimetre before lunging with lightning speed to surprise its prey.

Overleaf, right The strangely shaped hamerkop *(Scopus umbretta)* is well entrenched in local myth and superstition. In some regions, hamerkops are believed to be reincarnations of ancestors and are treated with immense respect.

LEFT Standing almost a metre-and-a-half high, the huge saddle-billed stork *(Ephippiorhynchus senegalensis)* preys mostly on large fish. Males and females can be distinguished by their eye colour – dark in males and yellow in females.

ABOVE Abdim's Stork *(Ciconia abdimii)* is a common non-breeding summer migrant from further north in Africa. Huge flocks, sometimes numbering thousands, can be found in grassland, field and savanna.

OPPOSITE The strangely shaped bill of the African open-billed stork *(Anastomus lamelligerus)* is superbly adapted for extracting the flesh from the aquatic snails and mussels that make up most of its diet. Because mussels can be particularly difficult to open, the storks sometimes leave theim lying in the sun until the mussel valves start to gape apart, after which the flesh can be scissored out with the tips of the mandibles.

LEFT AND TOP Yellow-billed storks *(Mycteria ibis)* are colonial breeders that make large stick nests in trees growing close to water. These storks are aquatic foragers and their range in southern Africa expands and contracts, depending on rainfall.

ABOVE The black stork *(Ciconia nigra)* is an uncommon resident which breeds on cliff faces or in caves in remote mountainous areas.

OPPOSITE Unlikely to win any beauty competitions, the marabou stork *(Leptoptilos crumeniferus)* nonetheless plays an important role as a carrion eater. It also has the greatest wingspan of any other flying bird in southern Africa.

TOP LEFT Although eastern white pelicans *(Pelecanus onocrotalus)* can become quite tame in urban environments, they are extremely sensitive to disturbance when breeding.

ABOVE Eastern white pelicans are 'pack hunters', forming a circle around shoals of fish and then converging together, sweeping the water with their huge, bag-like bill pouches. Although fish are their main food, they will also walk into colonies of gulls and cormorants, eating the young chicks as they go.

LEFT The all-dark beak of the lesser flamingo *(Phoenicopterus minor)* distinguishes it from its larger cousin, the greater flamingo *(P. ruber)*. Its diet comprises cyanobacteria (blue-green algae) from which it extracts the material it needs to synthesize the pink pigment that colours the feathers.

OPPOSITE Greater flamingos are long-lived birds that have very specialised requirements for breeding. Many of the breeding attempts in southern Africa fail because of rapidly falling water levels and a simultaneous crash in their shrimp food supply.

OVERLEAF LEFT The long, flattened bill of the African spoonbill *(Platalea alba)* is a special adaptation allowing it to sieve small, planktonic prey from the water.

OVERLEAF RIGHT The southern bald ibis *(Geronticus calvus)* is endemic to the high grasslands of eastern South Africa, Lesotho and Swaziland. It favours heavily grazed and recently burned areas.

LEFT The long-tailed, or reed cormorant *(Phalacrocorax africanus)* is a common resident of freshwater wetlands and watercourses. It feeds mostly on frogs and fish and breeds in colonies, frequently in association with herons, egrets and ibises.

ABOVE Over most of its African range, the white-breasted, or great cormorant *(P. carbo)* inhabits inland waterbodies. On the west coast, however, where the nutrient-rich waters of the Benguela Current support large stocks of fish, it breeds in colonies on the coast and at offshore islands.

OPPOSITE The sharp, dagger-like bill of the African darter *(Anhinga rufa)* – a resident of inland waters – is a highly effective underwater spear which it uses to impale its prey. It is often found at rivers and watercourses and, when swimming only its head and neck show above the surface of the water.

OPPOSITE The southern pochard *(Netta erythrophthalma)* has an interesting, disjunct distribution. It is found not only in sub-Saharan Africa, but also in South America.

BELOW The South African shelduck *(Tadorna cana)* is an endemic species. The head of the female (seen here) is white; that of the male is grey.

BOTTOM In some parts of South Africa, yellow-billed ducks *(Anas undulata)* are threatened by hybridisation with introduced mallards *(A. platyrhynchos).*

RIGHT The white-faced duck *(Dendrocygna viduata)* is a common and widespread species of the moist tropics and subtropics.

ABOVE The delicate Hottentot teal *(Anas hottentata)* is a shy species found mainly in quiet and secluded waterbodies. When breeding, it hides its waterside nest by creating a canopy from surrounding plants.

ABOVE In some parts of the region, numbers of Egyptian geese *(Alopochen aegyptiacus)* are increasing rapidly. These large flocks can cause considerable damage in croplands and research is under way to find means of reducing the farmers' losses.

OPPOSITE The diminutive pygmy goose *(Nettapus auritus)* often sits motionless among floating vegetation. It is a hole-nester, typically choosing a nest site in a dead tree, but sometimes selecting a termite mound or even an abandoned hamerkop nest.

LEFT In a unique fishing method, the lower mandible of the African skimmer *(Rhynchops flavirostris)* is 'trawled' through the water. When it touches prey, the bill snaps shut.
TOP The Caspian tern *(Hydroprogne caspia)* is the largest of the region's terns.
ABOVE The white-winged tern *(Chlidonias leucopterus)* is found largely around waterbodies but may venture further into the veld in search of insect food.
OPPOSITE In north temperate latitudes, great crested grebes *(Podiceps cristatus)* have distinct breeding and non-breeding plumages, losing the elaborate head pulmes in winter. In Africa, by contrast, they retain these plumes throughout the year.

LEFT Unlike any other southern African kingfisher, the pied kingfisher *(Ceryle rudis)* can hover above the water for extended periods in search of food. When rearing a brood of young, adults are sometimes assisted by the offspring of previous broods.

BELOW The brown-hooded kingfisher *(Halcyon albiventris)* is a terrestrial species of woodland and forest fringes. Unlike its fish-eating cousins, its diet is made up mostly of insects.

OPPOSITE The largest of the region's kingfishers, the giant kingfisher *(C. maxima)* weighs almost 30 times as much as the smallest species – the African pygmy kingfisher *(Isipina picta)*. The spotting on the upper breast identifies the bird shown here as a female.

OVERLEAF, LEFT Often providing no more of a view than a turquoise flash, the malachite kingfisher *(Alcedo cristata)* is fairly common at reed-fringed waterbodies and along well vegetated rivers.

OVERLEAF, RIGHT Similar in coloration to the malachite kingfisher, the pygmy kingfisher is the smallest of southern Africa's kingfishers. It is found mostly in savanna, wooded areas and well-treed coastal habitats.

TOP LEFT Holes in trees are the nesting sites of southern yellow-billed hornbills *(Tockus leucomelas)*. When the female is incubating, she uses material provided by the male to seal the nest entrance so that is almost closed and she is 'trapped' inside. Until 20 days after the first chick hatches, she is entirely dependent on her mate to provide food.

LEFT Red-billed hornbills *(T. erythrorhynchus)* frequently forage in groups, digging in the soil with their bills in search of insects, scorpions and seeds.

ABOVE Southern yellow-billed hornbills can become very tame, especially around camp sites and picnic areas in national parks.

OPPOSITE The southern yellow-billed hornbill is extremely catholic in its choice of food. Rodents, scorpions, centipedes and fruit all appear on the menu, and almost any suitably sized prey will be taken opportunistically.

LEFT Forests, woodland and thickets are home to the purple-crested lourie *(Tauraco porphyreolophus)*. The powerful, repetitive call is characteristic of the eastern lowlands.
BELOW The grey lourie *(Corythaixoides concolor)* is colloquially known as the 'go-away bird' because its persistent call readily translates as 'go-way'.
BOTTOM Meyer's parrot *(Poicephalus meyeri)* is fairly common in wooded savannas. Like most parrots, it is sociable and noisy, often forming flocks around waterholes.
OPPOSITE The South African range of the brown-headed parrot *(P. cryptoxanthus)* has contracted greatly in recent years, and Mozambique is now its regional stronghold.

TOP LEFT The Namaqua dove *(Oena capensis)* is common and wide-spread in arid habitats and undergoes considerable local movements.

LEFT Normally a shy, but vocal, inhabitant of woodlands, green-spotted doves *(Turtur chalcospilos)* can regularly be seen in the open as they come to waterholes to drink.

ABOVE Despite its electric coloration, the forest-dwelling Narina trogon *(Apaloderma narina)* is secretive and not easily seen.

OPPOSITE The African green pigeon *(Trevron calva)* neither sounds nor behaves like a typical pigeon. A group of these birds clambering around a fruit tree, frequently hanging upside down to reach a morsel, are much more reminiscent of parrots than pigeons.

OPPOSITE The crested barbet *(Trachyphonus vaillantii)* is common in the north and east. Its extended, trilling call is characteristic of wooded gardens.

BELOW The Diederik cuckoo *(Chrysococcyx caprius)* is a breeding summer migrant from tropical Africa that parasitizes several local species.

BOTTOM The red-fronted tinker barbet *(Pogoniulus pusillus)* is a common resident of east coast forests.

RIGHT The African hoopoe *(Upupa africana)* secretes a strong-smelling oil from its preen gland. The enclosed hole nest becomes extremely pungent and the powerful odour probably serves to deter predators.

TOP LEFT Arrow-marked babblers *(Turdoides jardineii)* are sociable and noisy. They are also a host of the striped cuckoo *(Clamator levaillantii)*. When the young cuckoo is begging for food, it makes a call almost identical to that of its foster parents.

LEFT The white-browed coucal *(Centropus superciliosus)* replaces Burchell's coucal *(C. burchellii)* in the extreme north of the region. Found in marshes and tall grass, its liquid, bubbling call is believed to presage rain.

ABOVE Burchell's starling *(Lamprotornis australis)* is found in fairly open, dry woodland and even in habitats as arid as the dry river beds of the Kalahari Desert.

OPPOSITE Meves' long-tailed starlings *(L. mevesii)* live and breed in groups. Within a group, only one pair will breed, but other group members, who are the young of previous years, will assist in raising the chicks.

ABOVE Although well adapted to life in the trees, Bennett's woodpeckers *(Campethera bennettii)* spend much of their time feeding on the ground, where ants form the major part of their diet.

TOP RIGHT Lilac-breasted rollers *(Coracias caudata)* are common in the northern parks of South Africa.

OPPOSITE Despite its name the purple roller *(Coracias naevia)* may be the least brightly coloured of the region's rollers, but makes up for this with spectacular rocking and rolling aerial displays interspersed with tumbling falls.

TOP LEFT Southern carmine bee-eaters *(Merops nubicoides)* visit here in summer to breed in colonies in river banks.
ABOVE Insects are the prey of southern carmine bee-eaters. They usually make sallying flights from a perch, but sometimes even perch on mammals and large birds such as Kori bustards, which they use as beaters to disturb insects.
LEFT Swallow-tailed bee-eaters *(M. hirundineus)* breed solitarily, excavating a long tunnel, often in quite flat ground. The eggs are laid in a chamber at the end of the tunnel.
OPPOSITE The white-fronted bee-eater *(M. bullockoides)* is typically a bird of riverine and lakeshore woodland. Its range does, however, extend west into the arid regions.

ABOVE Although the bill and tongue of the greater double-collared sunbird *(Nectarina afra)* are well adapted for nectar-feeding, spiders plucked from their webs, form an important part of the diet.

ABOVE If a scarlet-chested sunbird *(N. senegalensis)* cannot reach a flower's nectar by probing, it resorts to piercing the base of the flower. Although this provides food for the sunbird, it has no pollination benefit for the plant.

ABOVE The white-bellied sunbird *(N. talatala)* underatkes seasonal movements to avoid the extremes of arid winters.
OPPOSITE The Cape sugarbird *(Promerops cafer)* is confined to the Cape Floral Kingdom in the extreme south west.

FAR LEFT The spotted-backed weaver *(Ploceus cucullatus)* is gregarious and is usually found close to water, especially when breeding.

LEFT When finished, the nest of the Cape weaver *(P. capensis)* will have a long, downward-pointing entrance funnel.

ABOVE Thick-billed weavers *(Amblyospiza albifrons)* breed in reedbeds, but spend most of the year feeding in forests.

OPPOSITE The southern masked weaver *(P. velatus)* is by far the most widespread weaver of the region. It is a true habitat generalist, avoiding only evergreen forests.

ABOVE The tail plumes of the male long-tailed widow *(Euplectus progne)* attract females but – to assist flying and avoid predation – they are moulted out at the end of the breeding season.

ABOVE The male eastern paradise whydah *(Vidua paradisaea);* the female is a brood parasite, laying its eggs in the nests of the melba finch *(Pytilia melba).*

ABOVE It is only during the breeding season that the golden bishop *(Euplectes afer)* sports dazzling black-and-yellow plumage.

ABOVE The resplendent breeding dress of the male red bishop *(E. orix)* belies the damage that huge flocks of these birds can cause to grain crops.

OPPOSITE Unlike most shrikes, the long-tailed shrike *(Corvinella melanoleuca)* is gregarious and is almost invariably found in small groups of up to 10 or 12 birds.
BELOW In the arid sandy savannas, the Kalahari robin *(Erythropygia paena)* spends much of its time searching for food on the ground.
BOTTOM The buff-streaked chat *(Oenanthe bifasciata)* is endemic to the grasslands of eastern South Africa, where it favours rocky slopes.
RIGHT The common fiscal shrike *(Lanius collaris)* is a familiar sight throughout most of the region. This bird's white eye-stripe identifies it as coming from the arid west.

ABOVE The yellow canary *(Serinus flaviventris)* is primarily a bird of the arid west. It can be found in flocks throughout the Karoo and Namaqualand, often mixing with other seed-eaters.

ABOVE CENTRE The Cape white-eye *(Zosterops pallidus)* is an abundant resident in the south and west. It is a common garden bird, frequently becoming very tame.

ABOVE RIGHT The name of the bokmakierie *(Telophorus zeylonus)* is a rendition of the duet it sings. At the onset of the breeding season, the dry western scrublands echo to the bokmakieries' diverse vocal repertoire.

OPPOSITE Red-headed finches *(Amadina erythrocephala)* frequently take over disused nests of other birds, to which they add some lining of their own. In Namibia, the nests of chestnut weavers *(Ploceus rubiginosus)* are a favourite.

OVERLEAF, LEFT Evergreen forest and riverine bush are the natural home of the olive thrush *(Turdus olivaceus)*. However, it has expanded its range by adapting well to parks, suburban gardens and plantations.

OVERLEAF, RIGHT The sentinel rock thrush *(Monticola explorator)* is primarily a species of montane grassland and fynbos, but many kinds descend to lower altitudes in the winter months.

LEFT The well-camouflaged nest of the African paradise flycatcher *(Terpsiphone viridis)* is a neatly woven structure, bound with spiders' web and decorated with lichen.

TOP The ashy tit *(Parus cinerascens)* is a noisy resident of the dry western savannas. It nests in holes in trees and sometimes roosts at night in the nests of sociable weavers.

ABOVE The red-billed firefinch *(Lagonosticta senegala)*, shown here, escapes parasitism by the steel-blue widowfinch *(Vidua chalybeata)* only in the extreme south west of its range.

OPPOSITE The Cape reed warbler *(Acrocephalus gracilirostris)* is a skulking resident of tall reedbeds. These birds sometimes occur at high densities, as evidenced by the cacophony of singing males in the breeding season.

OVERLEAF Red-billed oxpeckers *(Buphagus africanus)* have specially modified feet and bills that allow them to cling to the hides of animals in order to glean parasites.